IT'S TIME TO LEARN ABOUT CERATOSAURUSES

It's Time to Learn about Ceratosauruses

Walter the Educator

Silent King Books
A WhichHead Entertainment Imprint

Copyright © 2025 by Walter the Educator

All rights reserved. No part of this book may be reproduced in any manner whatsoever without written per- mission except in the case of brief quotations embodied in critical articles and reviews.

First Printing, 2024

Disclaimer

This book is a literary work; the story is not about specific persons, locations, situations, and/or circumstances unless mentioned in a historical context. Any resemblance to real persons, locations, situations, and/or circumstances is coincidental. This book is for entertainment and informational purposes only. The author and publisher offer this information without warranties expressed or implied. No matter the grounds, neither the author nor the publisher will be accountable for any losses, injuries, or other damages caused by the reader's use of this book. The use of this book acknowledges an understanding and acceptance of this disclaimer.

It's Time to Learn about Ceratosauruses is a collectible early learning book by Walter the Educator suitable for all ages belonging to Walter the Educator's Time to Eat Book Series. Collect more books at WaltertheEducator.com

USE THE EXTRA SPACE TO TAKE NOTES AND DOCUMENT YOUR MEMORIES

CERATOSAURUSES

Long ago in days of old,

It's Time to Learn about
Ceratosauruses

A dinosaur so fierce and bold,

With teeth so sharp and claws so strong,

Ceratosaurus walked along.

With sturdy legs and mighty tail,

It stomped through forests without fail.

Through rivers deep and trees so tall,

It roamed and ruled among them all.

Upon its head, a horn so bright,

A special mark, a fearsome sight!

Some say for show, some say for fight,

It made this dino stand out right.

Its body long, its arms so small,

Yet strong enough to help it brawl.

With razor teeth and eyes so keen,

It was a hunter, quick and mean.

It's Time to Learn about
Ceratosauruses

Meat it craved, a carnivore,

It hunted food and wanted more.

With mighty jaws, it bit down fast,

Its meal was caught, it didn't last!

It shared its time with others grand,

Like Allosaurs upon the land.

But though they both were big and strong,

Ceratosaurus didn't belong.

For it was special, sleek and light,

A dino built to chase and fight.

With speed and power, smart and sly,

It ruled the land, the lakes nearby.

Jurassic times were wild and wide,

But Ceratosaurus took great stride.

Through swamp and plain, it left its mark,

It's Time to Learn about
Ceratosauruses

Its roaring voice both loud and stark.

Then time moved on, the world did change,

The earth grew different, vast, and strange.

The dinosaurs all disappeared,

But in the rocks, their bones appeared.

Now we learn from what we find,

A glimpse of life they left behind.

Ceratosaurus, strong and true,

It's Time to Learn about
Ceratosauruses

A dinosaur to learn and view!

ABOUT THE CREATOR

Walter the Educator is one of the pseudonyms for Walter Anderson. Formally educated in Chemistry, Business, and Education, he is an educator, an author, a diverse entrepreneur, and he is the son of a disabled war veteran. "Walter the Educator" shares his time between educating and creating. He holds interests and owns several creative projects that entertain, enlighten, enhance, and educate, hoping to inspire and motivate you. Follow, find new works, and stay up to date with Walter the Educator™ at WaltertheEducator.com

www.ingramcontent.com/pod-product-compliance
Lightning Source LLC
LaVergne TN
LVHW051920060526
838201LV00060B/4087